PIANO/VOCAL SELECTIONS

THE NEIL DIAMOND MUSICAL
A BEAUTIFUL NOISE

T0051690

ISBN 978-1-70518-902-3

Visit Hal Leonard Online at
www.halleonard.com

World headquarters, contact:
Hal Leonard
7777 West Bluemound Road
Milwaukee, WI 53213
Email: info@halleonard.com

In Europe, contact:
Hal Leonard Europe Limited
1 Red Place
London, W1K 6PL
Email: info@halleonardeurope.com

In Australia, contact:
Hal Leonard Australia Pty. Ltd.
4 Lentara Court
Cheltenham, Victoria, 3192 Australia
Email: info@halleonard.com.au

AMERICA

Words and Music by
NEIL DIAMOND

Ev-'ry-where a - round__ the world,

they're com - ing to A - mer - i - ca. Ev - 'ry time__ that flag's_

__ un - furled,_ they're com - ing to A - mer - i - ca.

Repeat and Fade

BEAUTIFUL NOISE

Words and Music by
NEIL DIAMOND

CRACKLIN' ROSIE

Words and Music by
NEIL DIAMOND

FOREVER IN BLUE JEANS

Words and Music by NEIL DIAMOND
and RICHARD BENNETT

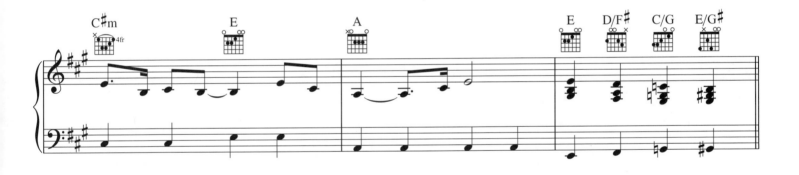

Mon - ey talks. But it don't sing and dance, and it don't walk.

HELLO AGAIN

Words by NEIL DIAMOND
Music by NEIL DIAMOND
and ALAN LINDGREN

HOLLY HOLY

Words and Music by
NEIL DIAMOND

Hol - hol-ly ho - ly rain.

Hol - ly ho - ly

love.

8vb

I AM...I SAID

Words and Music by
NEIL DIAMOND

and then be-came one? ____ Well, ex- cept for the names ____ and a few oth-er chang - es, if you talk a-bout me, ____ the sto-ry's the same one. But I got an emp-ti-ness deep in - side. ____ And I've tried, ____ but it won't let me

LOVE ON THE ROCKS

Words and Music by NEIL DIAMOND
and GILBERT BECAUD

SEPTEMBER MORN

Words and Music by NEIL DIAMOND
and GILBERT BECAUD

SHILO

Words and Music by
NEIL DIAMOND

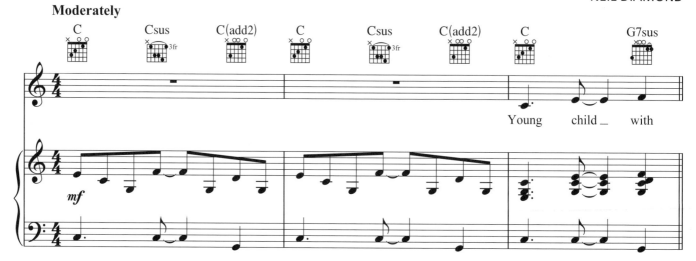

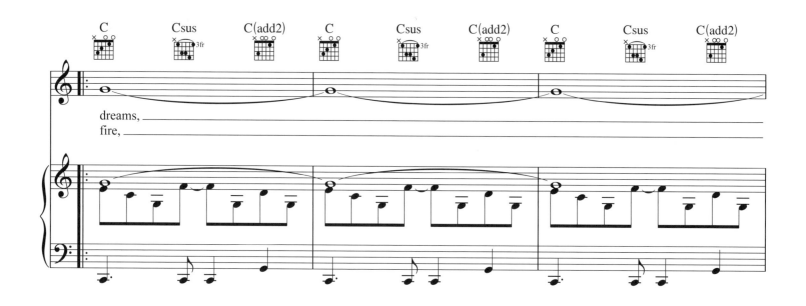

SOLITARY MAN

Words and Music by
NEIL DIAMOND

SONG SUNG BLUE

Words and Music by
NEIL DIAMOND

Song sung blue, ev-'ry-bod-y knows one.

Song sung blue, ev-'ry gar-den grows one.

and be-fore you know it start to feel-in' good. ___ You sim-ply got no choice. ___

YOU DON'T BRING ME FLOWERS

Words by NEIL DIAMOND,
MARILYN BERGMAN and ALAN BERGMAN
Music by NEIL DIAMOND

Slowly and freely

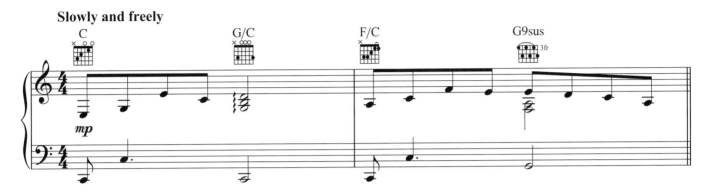

You don't bring me flow-ers; you don't sing me love songs.

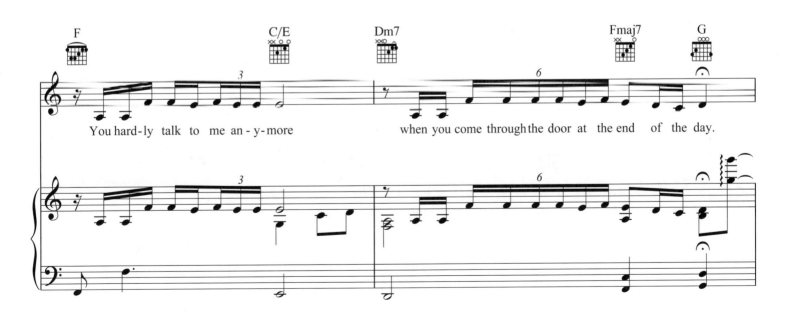

You hard-ly talk to me an-y-more when you come through the door at the end of the day.

SWEET CAROLINE

Words and Music by
NEIL DIAMOND

Moderately, very steady

Where it be-gan, ___

I can't be-gin to know-in', but then I